IMAGES
of America

BRIDGEPORT

IMAGES
of America

BRIDGEPORT

Judy Barrett

ARCADIA
PUBLISHING

Published by Arcadia Publishing
Charleston, South Carolina

Library of Congress Control Number: 2013945004

For all general information, please contact Arcadia Publishing:
Telephone 843-853-2070
Fax 843-853-0044
E-mail sales@arcadiapublishing.com
For customer service and orders:
Toll-Free 1-888-313-2665

Visit us on the Internet at www.arcadiapublishing.com

*To all the people of Bridgeport whose story sharing and photographs
made this book a reality; to all the ancestors of Bridgeport
people who paved the way for life in this community*

CONTENTS

Acknowledgments   6

Introduction   7

1.   Bridges   9

2.   Businesses and Homes Along Route 31   15

3.   People and Families   29

4.   Oneida Lake Bays and Points   35

5.   Oneida Lake Activities and Scenery   55

6.   Farms   65

7.   Along Bridgeport Roads   91

8.   Places People Gather   101

ACKNOWLEDGMENTS

So many people—well over 50—have shared their photographs and, more importantly, their stories of life in Bridgeport. When I met with them to see their photographs, our conversations were always very long. People were incredibly helpful and generous with their time. Whether you shared one photograph or several, it all went together to create a story of our beloved community. Unless otherwise noted, all images come from the author's collection.

I would like to especially thank Judy Shepard for the giving of her time and talent in typing the captions. Thank you, Karen Miller, Sandra Bushnell Wilsey, and Pamela Vittorio, for sharing so many stories and research skills. My relatives Nancy, Bruce, and Robert were extremely helpful with the sharing of their computer skills. I must also thank Arcadia Publishing for making a long-standing wish come true to share the story of Bridgeport. A final but very special thank-you goes to my acquisitions editor at Arcadia, Rémy Thurston. He used a great deal of time and patience to explicitly explain to me how to make this book become a reality.

INTRODUCTION

Settlers came to the area of Bridgeport and Chittenango Creek as early as 1802. Much about the early settlers is contained in two early histories of Madison County, one written by Mrs. L.M. Hammond in 1872 and one edited by John E. Smith in 1899. Stories handed down for generations tell of the interaction between the first settlers and the Native Americans in the area. Capt. Robert Barnes is considered by some historians to be the first settler. Another local pioneer was Levi Jennings. A Mr. Rector, another early settler, had a farm that was close to the creek and had many dealings with the Native Americans.

There are also three or four other histories written by local people that tell the record and sometimes the folklore of the community. Probably the most reliable was written by David H. Brown, who lived in Bridgeport all of his life, from 1838 to 1906. Some of the information in this introduction comes from that source.

In the days before written history, Native Americans used Oneida Lake and Chittenango Creek as food sources and very often camped out on the shores of both in the summer months. Many remnants of their being here have been found, especially by farmers plowing their fields. There have been historical references to both the Oneida and the Tuscarora tribes. They were part of the Six Nation Iroquois Confederacy. The Turtle Tree Incident, involving the Tuscarora Nation, occurred along Chittenango Creek in 1776.

From the early 1800s on, settlers began to arrive in the area, quite logically settling along Chittenango Creek, which provided a source of food and an easy way to travel to Oneida Lake. As farms developed in the area and to provide needed products for the farms, many small businesses were created in the hamlet near the creek and along the road that later became Route 31.

There has always been much discussion as to when the first bridge was built in Bridgeport. As small businesses were developed on both sides of the creek, they first had to ford the creek, usually by horseback. This could be difficult in the early-spring flooding times. According to information in the New York State Archives, a span over Chittenango Creek at Bridgeport was constructed sometime prior to July 1819, when the bridge is mentioned in the boundary description of a survey map for the Westmoreland Sodus Bay Turnpike Company created by Barnet Mooney and James Adams.

Another much-debated topic is where Bridgeport got its name. Some believe it was because some of the early settlers came from areas near Bridgeport, Connecticut. Others feel it was because of the early bridges that were so essential to the development of the community.

One of the first businesses was a sawmill, as farmers needed lumber to build homes and barns. Trees were cut down and brought to the mill, where they were sawed into boards. Sometimes, if the trees were cut down near the creek, logs were floated to the sawmill.

Because the sawmill and other businesses needed a source of power, a bridge was constructed with a dam. The resulting waterpower was converted into the necessary power to run the grain grinders to get work done. Because of all the farms in the area, a gristmill was opened. Farmers brought their wheat and oats to be ground and used to make animal feed, bread, and baked goods.

Another early business was a tannery, which tanned animal hides to be made into harnesses, boots, and shoes. Along the creek and what was later Route 31, there were businesses that made shoes, pegs, matches, cigars, and barrels. In later years, many barrels were sold to the Syracuse Salt Works in Syracuse. Also in the 1800s, Loren Damon was building boats in a barn on Route 31.

A post office opened in Bridgeport as early as the mid-1800s. Some of the early postmasters were a Mr. Rector, a Mr. Cook, and a Mr. Conklin. From 1898 until 1945, the post office was located in the D.H. Brown store. Many different people served as postmasters during that time. After that, the post office moved to many different locations.

The roads in the village were made by a path maker. His job was to keep the ruts out of the early dirt road. Later, a water-bound road was built. Two layers of crushed stone were put on the road. A newspaper photograph from 1912 shows this process on Route 31.

There have been many grocery and general stores in early Bridgeport and over the years. D.H. Brown & Sons, the Bridgeport Cash Store, which was later Lulu VanAlstyne's store, the Kneeskern store, and many other small stores served locals. Much later, there were stores owned by Richard Brown, Harold Ferstler, Frank Vavonese, and Ed Young.

Bridgeport had two hotels on Route 31 for many years. The Sternberg Hotel began around 1850. It had several owners and different names over the years. The building is still in operation as a bar and grill on the corner of Route 31 and Bridgeport-Kirkville Road. Between that road and the creek was the Slingerland Hotel, which had several other names and was destroyed by a fire in 1935.

Probably the largest source of income for the above-mentioned businesses came from local farmers. In this book, 40 to 50 farms are highlighted. Over the years, there were even more. However, Bridgeport's farms slowly disappeared, as did many of the businesses already mentioned. Today, there are still a few enterprises on the east side of the creek, mostly along Route 31. They include a bicycle shop, two car repair businesses, a liquor store, three beauty shops, a recycling center, a lawyer's office, several used-car lots, a restaurant, and a hardware store. On the west side of the creek are a diner, Kinney Drugs, a Dunkin' Donuts, a Subway, a Dollar General, a Laundromat, a pizza place, and a funeral home.

Bridgeport has become a commuter residential area. Most residents have jobs in the general Syracuse area. In Cicero and Dewitt, there are many large chain grocery stores and other businesses, and residents of Bridgeport can stop on the way home from work to do their shopping. Many beautiful homes have been built in the area and along the lakeshore. People can enjoy the peace of country living but also have access to city goods. Who could ask for more?

One

BRIDGES

Chittenango Creek has always played a vital role in the history of the hamlet of Bridgeport. The first white settlers arrived around 1802. During the very early history of the hamlet, a bridge was constructed across the creek, connecting Madison and Onondaga Counties. The bridge is mentioned in a July 1819 survey map (supplied to the author courtesy of Sandra Wilsey) for the Westmoreland Sodus Bay Turnpike Company. The map was created by Barnet Mooney and James Adams and refers to the bridge in the map's boundary description. The creek runs north into Oneida Lake. (Courtesy of Carol Greene.)

Seen here is the first bridge, built with a dam. The dam provided power to operate a granary on the east bank of the creek. There was a sawmill on the west side of the creek that likely also tapped into the power of the dam. The photograph below shows people on the bridge. Early locals surely fished off the span, as they still do today. The granary is on the left of the image. The building on the right has a porch and was probably one of the early hotels along Route 31. (Above, courtesy of Carol Greene; below, courtesy of Karen Miller.)

BRIDGEPORT, N.Y.

The dam was eventually removed, and, over the years, the foundation for the bridge began to deteriorate. It was repaired and then eventually taken down. The low bridge seen here was constructed across the creek as a temporary solution until the new span was completed. The low water level made that solution possible. (Courtesy of Raymond and Joyce Damon.)

NEW BRIDGE -BRIDGEPORT, N.Y.

In 1909–1910, a new, much more modern truss bridge was constructed. Once again, the granary and other businesses are visible on the east side of the bridge. Eventually, as cars were made wider and trucks needed to pass over the bridge, it became very difficult for the drivers of these vehicles. Often, traffic could only go in one direction at a time. (Courtesy of Richard Strong.)

The bridge seen here was built in 1939. It was wide enough for two cars to cross at a time. The old granary burned down and was replaced with the building on the left. Also on the left is the Esso gas station. The building on the right was eventually a bar and restaurant. At one time, it was called the Bridgeport Inn. (Courtesy of Thomas Mafrici.)

The latest bridge is seen here under construction in 1998–1999. The old bridge continued to be used during this time. The new span included sidewalks on both sides, running east to North Road and west on Route 31. (Courtesy of Della Detore.)

Two

BUSINESSES AND HOMES
ALONG ROUTE 31

This area has been referred to as Cook's Corner for many years. The first house on the left belonged to R.O. Cook, a teacher at the Bridgeport two-room schoolhouse. He would sit in the front of the house every day and write notes about what went on in Bridgeport. Some people in the community still have those original pages. The small house between Cook's house and the Slingerland Hotel was once a hat shop. Later, the Jardine family lived in it, before eventually moving to Cook's house. Note the Socony gas station beyond the hotel. (Courtesy of Carol Greene.)

Here is another image of Main Street. The hotel was still there then, but this photograph was taken before the gas station was built. Note the people standing on the hotel steps and the hand pump for water, just past the sign. The street is not yet paved. Years later, in January 1935, the hotel burned to the ground. It was called the Cowan Hotel at the time. (Courtesy of Carol Greene.)

After the original hotel burned, the property was bought by Charles Arney. It was used as a store and a gas station when this photograph was taken, after the road was paved. In later years, Arney's son-in-law, Don Moyer, had a barbershop in the front of the store. (Courtesy of Dawn Pindle Falge.)

Eventually, the Arney store was purchased by Lyle and Dolly Sattler. The store and garage were a Western Auto franchise. The little house next to what used to be the Cook house was moved elsewhere in town, but people still living in Bridgeport cannot agree exactly where it was moved. The home of R.O. Cook was later owned by the Jardine family. At one time, Mary Jardine had a gift shop in the front part of the house. At this time, there is a beauty shop there. To the right of Western Auto is the home of the Frank Pindle family. (Courtesy of Donald and Mary Sattler.)

Loren Damon and his son Ceylon built the famous Damon boats in the barn behind the family house (above) on Route 31. Later, Loren's grandson Ronald joined the business. At left, Ronald Damon sits in a Damon boat in the 1920s. (Above, courtesy of Raymond and Joyce Damon; left, courtesy of Karen Miller.)

 *Building*  *Repairing*

DAMON'S BOATS

"Built to Endure"

OUTBOARDS ～ ROWBOATS ～ SPEED BOATS

C. N. DAMON   Bridgeport, N. Y.

The Damon boatbuilders used this card to advertise their business. Note the "Built to Endure" slogan. There are still a few Damon boats around today. The Damons began building them in the late 1800s and continued the business until the 1920s. It was said that a Damon boat never sank on Oneida Lake. (Courtesy of Karen Miller.)

This is a winter scene of Route 31 in Bridgeport. It was taken after 1910, as it shows the new hotel, by then called the Bridgeport Inn. In later years, a different Bridgeport Inn that was operated by the Koegel family was in the building right next to the creek, down the road. (Courtesy of Karen Miller.)

This photograph shows the same bridge and granary seen on the previous page. However, the sign on this building now reads "Miller Tires." The building to the left of Route 31 was once the Terpenny store. Much later, it became the Koegel's Bridgeport Inn. (Courtesy of Carol Greene.)

Vic Dean Sr. is seen here in front of his home, which was also the first location of the Dean bait shop. Dean lived across the street from the creek, on what was first called Tuft Street and is now Green Street. (Courtesy of Bonnie Dean Gallouresi.)

The first house in this image belonged to Vic Dean Jr. He also ran a bait shop on Tufts Street. The lower part of the house was the bait shop, and the family lived upstairs. The white house belonged to Harry and Sadie Sheldon. One of their sons, Thomas, became an educator and then the assistant to the New York director of education in Albany. (Courtesy of Bonnie Dean Gallouresi.)

Stamberg Hotel - Bridgeport, N. Y.

This photograph shows another very old hotel in Bridgeport, the Sternberg Hotel (spelled incorrectly on this card). Through the years, the hotel had many names, including the Nichols, the Days, the Union, the Bottings, and Teddy's Hotel. The present owners have changed the name back to the Union Hotel. Their sign indicates it was founded in 1856. In 1944, the roof of the building collapsed from the weight of too much snow. (Courtesy of Carol Greene.)

There were many businesses along Route 31. This image shows another very snowy day. The building to the left was once the Bridgeport Cash Store, run by Albert Dunham. It later became known as Lulu's store, run by Lulu VanAlstyne. It was a favorite for kids to visit, as she always handed out penny candies to them. Lulu sold many things, from thread and material to canned goods. Across North Road was the Ames house, which was previously owned by Pat Briggs. That building was moved over to the right when the new Methodist church was built on that corner. The old Methodist church on North Road had burned. (Courtesy of Deb Honors.)

The D.H. Brown store was in Bridgeport on Route 31 for years. It was run by two brothers, Dick and David Brown. The original store building was converted from an old wagon factory in 1882. The Bridgeport Post Office was in the store for a very long time. Old-timers would sit around the stove in the middle of the store and chat after they had picked up their mail and finished their shopping. The image below shows Alley's Custard Stand, across the street and east of the Brown store. This was a favorite spot to get a yummy custard cone, as well as hamburgers, hot dogs, and soda. The building to the right was a gas station run by Jim Alley, and the building to the left was the family home. Just beyond that is the edge of the old Bridgeport Opera House, later known as the Bridgeport Playhouse. (Above, courtesy of Carol Greene; below, courtesy of Sharon Alley Sattler.)

One day in the late 1940s or early 1950s, a man from Canada was driving through the hamlet with his animals on a tour around the country. He was allowed to let the animals stretch out and rest in the field behind Alley's. This photograph shows a moose. The man also had a bear, a wolf, and a fox. Many people came to Alley's to see the animals. They bought all the food that was available in the store in one day. (Courtesy of Sharon Alley Sattler.)

The Tydol gas station was located on Route 31, just before the Bitz farm. G.R. Sayles opened it in 1930 or 1931. Over the years, the little building has been the location of many different establishments. It still stands today; most recently, used cars were sold there. (Courtesy of Barbara Block.)

Greentree Nursery is seen here. The Kneeskerns, Alice and Irwin, ran the nursery behind their home. They lived on the corner of Route 31 and Weaver Road, in a house often called "the Gingerbread House." In the spring and summer, it was a popular place to buy trees and plants. (Courtesy of Carolyn Nojaim.)

The Madison Motel, seen here in the 1950s, was located on the corner of Route 31 and Tyler Road, just east of the hamlet. The popular motel included a bar and, sometimes, a restaurant in the 1950s. (Courtesy of Carol Greene.)

Three

PEOPLE AND FAMILIES

In 1948, Edward and Loretta Myers had come to visit at Edith and Robert Cooper's home on Bridgeport-Kirkville Road. Several Cooper families lived on that same road. More than five generations of Coopers have lived in Bridgeport. Note the clock on the garage, which came from a diner that used to be next to the granary on Route 31. It was reportedly lighted each night. (Courtesy of Cece Shiavone.)

Blondelia "Blondie" Collar Damon (left) is seen here with a friend. Blondie married Leon Damon around 1930, and they lived on the farm on Damon's Point. Blondie's mother was Leah Brown Collar, the sister of the owners of the Brown store. (Courtesy of Raymond and Joyce Damon.)

This is a tintype of Edmond Damon, who was born in Bridgeport in 1809. He constructed the cobblestone house on Route 31. When he built it, there were no trees or houses between it and Oneida Lake. All of the stones were brought from the lake to the building site. His two sisters helped him move them. (Courtesy of Karen Miller.)

Here, the Kneeskern family enjoys a picnic under the shade trees around the Gothic-style home known as "the Gingerbread House." It is located at the corner of Route 31 and Weaver Road. They are probably taking a break from working at the nursery they ran behind the house. (Courtesy of Caroline Nojaim.)

This early cycler is Doris Palmer, the sister of Floyd and Frank Palmer. She lived on the Palmer farm, on Route 31 near Tyler Road. This photograph was taken in 1915. Doris married Minor Bitz, and they were the parents of Shirley Pooley. (Courtesy of Jean Prawl.)

Rose Brown and some young boys are seen here in the early 1900s. Some of the boys are, in no particular order, Richard Brown, Buster Brown, Gilbert Slingerland, and Dean Damon. They are sitting on the porch of the Slingerland Hotel. (Courtesy of Deb Honors.)

These four Brown cousins are the children of David and Rose Brown and Dick and Ella Brown. The children are, from left to right, Buster, Richard, Dortha, and Bill. Buster and Bill are David's children, and Richard and Dortha are Dick's children. This photograph was taken soon after Bill was born in 1909. (Courtesy of Hollis Strong.)

Dortha and Richard Brown are the children of Dick and Ella Brown. Dortha's married name was Strong. Richard went into the grocery store business, as his father had. Later, he was elected to the state assembly. (Courtesy of Raymond and Joyce Damon.)

David Holland Brown Sr. lived from 1837 to 1906. He was the father of David H. Brown and Richard Brown Sr., who both ran the D.H. Brown general store. Brown Sr. originally operated a wagon and cutter factory, which was later converted into the general store. (Courtesy of Raymond and Joyce Damon.)

Three young cyclists are seen here near the intersection of Route 31 and North Road in 1918. They are, from left to right, Donald Dunham, Francis Pindle, and Elmer Slingerland. In the background is the store that was known as the Bridgeport Cash Store and then Lulu's store, located on the corner of Route 31 and North Road. (Courtesy of William Pindle.)

Levi Jennings was a very early settler in Bridgeport. Members of the Jennings family today say that he lived in this home somewhere on the Shackelton Point Road. In some histories, he is mentioned as helping to build a dam across the creek, and then he ran the gristmill powered by the dam. (Courtesy of Janice Lindsey.)

Four

ONEIDA LAKE
BAYS AND POINTS

For many years, Floyd Palmer (right) had a camp on Hitchcock Point, giving him access to Oneida Lake. He is seen here showing off his great catch of fish with his friend George Terrance. There is and always has been good fishing on the lake. Bass, perch, walleye, bullheads, and pike are all available for a good fisherman. (Courtesy of Jean Prawl.)

Floyd Palmer (right) and Ed McDonald show off their goose-hunting skills. In the fall, many geese and ducks fly through the area, and hunters are busy. In the background on the edge of the lake is a duck blind. Hunters build them with evergreen boughs all around a wooden base so they can hide until the birds get close enough to shoot. (Courtesy of Jean Prawl.)

This photograph was taken off of Hitchcock Point, with Damon Point in the background. This deer had swum across the lake and was too afraid and exhausted to get out of the water. These men went out in their boats to coax it to shore so it could rest and then be on its way. (Courtesy of Jean Prawl.)

The James McDonald building is still a camp on Andrews Shore Road near Hitchcock Point. It was built in 1942–1943. The family keeps it simple and rustic to this day. It has never been lived in year-round, but they have always enjoyed coming to it in the summer. The building nearest the road is where all the cooking is done. In the McDonald family, there were ten girls and one boy, making for a jam-packed little camp at bedtime. The mosquitoes were very bad, coming from the wooded area behind the camp. In the fall, the men in the family often came out to the camp to hunt or fish on Oneida Lake. (Courtesy of Sally [McDonald] Seeley.)

Lee Weeks bought lakefront property on Fisher Bay from John Barrett around 1938. The property had 300 feet of lake frontage. Weeks built a cottage that the family spent many summers enjoying. Around 1950, he sold the cottage. This photograph shows the back of the cottage with Brad Weeks next to the 1945 car. (Courtesy of Bradford Weeks.)

This is the back of the camp belonging to Harriett Willey and her mother, Hattie Byrnes, on Fisher Bay. They purchased the property in 1946, when Harriett's son Carlton was eight years old. They used the camp for many years. When Carlton married, he built a year-round home on the property. (Courtesy of Ann Willey.)

This is a family picnic at a camp on the Conrad Fisher farm property. The clothing likely dates the photograph to the early 1920s. At that time, people did not use the type of picnic tables regularly used today; they just brought tables and chairs outside. Of course, everyone brought his or her food specialty to share.

Tony Ross of Ross' Bakery in Syracuse owned a camp on Fisher Bay. He and his wife, Ange, are seen here in their beautiful Chris-Craft boat, which was named *Ange*. Everyone loved it when Tony came home from work at night, as he would bring the leftover donuts and breads to share with his neighbors. (Courtesy of Joan Laura.)

Tony Ross always put on a show with his Chris-Craft. He is seen here towing his daughter on water skis in 1948. At the time, this was not a common activity on the lake. (Courtesy of Joan Laura.)

Bev Weeks stands on the deck in front of her family's camp on Fisher Bay, showing off a nice catch of fish. It would be rare to see a girl that age catch so many fish today, especially while wearing a dress. (Courtesy of Bradford Weeks.)

In the center distance of this image is the first camp ever on Damon's Point. It was built by a man from Syracuse who owned a furniture store. He did not own the land the camp was on; instead, he leased it from Leon Damon, who had a farm there. (Courtesy of Raymond and Joyce Damon.)

Over the years, more and more people leased land from Leon Damon and built camps. This went on for many years, with the campers paying a lease fee. Some people stayed in the camps all summer and commuted to work. Others came to camp on weekends or for vacations. (Courtesy of Arlene Keppler.)

Leon Damon and his wife, Blondie, ran a store across the street from their farmhouse. Kids were especially happy to buy ice cream there. On Saturday nights, dances were held inside the building. The store surely closed for the winter, as few people had year-round homes there. (Courtesy of Raymond and Joyce Damon.)

In the 1940s, this camp belonged to the Nutting family. They took it over from the person who built the first camp on Damon's Point. At that time, they still had to pay a lease fee for the property the camp was on, as it belonged to Leon Damon, who lived on and owned the farm that made up the Damon's Point property. Eventually, all the campers there were allowed to purchase the properties their buildings sat on. Many of the camps were then converted into year-round homes. The early campers came for the summer to go fishing, boating, or swimming. In the winter, they would return to the camps to go skating or ice fishing on the lake. The photograph below shows the hand pump that, in the early days, was the only source of drinking water for campers on Damon's Point. (Both, courtesy of Alan Nutting.)

There were several roads off of Damon Point Road, where more land was leased and more camps were built. These camps were on very small lots and very close together. As time went on, many of the camps were winterized and made into year-round homes. Some were torn down and replaced by new residences. People wanted to have access to the lake for fishing, in both the summer and the winter. Many of these homes face Billington Bay. On a sunny summer weekend, the bay is full of people out on their boats, eating, swimming, or water-skiing. In the winter, there are many snowmobiles riding on the lake and people ice fishing. (Above, courtesy of Carol Greene; below, courtesy of Arlene Keppler.)

Damon Point Road leads straight to the lake. There are no camps or houses there, but there are many boats and people, as seen here. The view in this photograph looks out at the lake and Shackelton Point in the distance. (Courtesy of Jean Prawl.)

Damon's Point is seen here in winter. The high snowbanks show how deep the snow must have been before the snowplow came through. The children could go sledding or make a snow fort. Sometimes, parents and children built fires and roasted marshmallows together. (Courtesy of Patricia Hogan.)

This camp was built on Pierce Road, on Oneida Lake, in the late 1800s. The property had been part of the Billington farm, on Shackelton Point Road. It was a summer camp, but campers often came out to do winter sports. Frank Greiner is seen here with his girlfriend in the 1930s. He has snowshoes over his shoulder that he used to keep from sinking too deeply in the snow. The camp was originally owned by Greiner and John Haar, who are both relatives of Martha Greiner Eischen. Martha and her husband, Francis, tore down an old camp there and built a year-round home on the same road. (Courtesy of Francis and Martha Eischen.)

This is the Groesbeck farmhouse. It was near Shackelton Point, but not on the lake. The Groesbecks lived here until around 1920, running a dairy farm. The whole area was wide-open pastureland with a few trees. (Courtesy of Cornell University Biological Field Station.)

The barn and milk house on the Groesbeck dairy farm are seen here around 1930. (Courtesy of Cornell University Biological Field Station.)

In the mid-to-late-1800s, Charles Shackelton established the Shackelton Hotel. It was set back from the water and had a beautiful view of the lake, Briggs Bay, and Dutchman's Island. It was considered an Oneida Lake resort. (Courtesy of Cornell University Biological Field Station.)

SHACKELTON'S POINT - ONEIDA LAKE -

In 1887, Charles Shackelton decided to enhance his property on the point by developing it with fine cottages. The cottages were along the shoreline facing east. They had porches and were amongst beautiful shade trees. Below, ladies are out enjoying a beautiful summer day. A steamboat landing was also built for the use of the campers. (Above, courtesy of the Cornell University Biological Field Station; below, courtesy of Carol Greene.)

SHERMAN'S VIEW - SHACKELTON'S POINT - ONEIDA LAKE

49

WEBBER'S VIEW - SHACKELTON'S POINT - ONEIDA LAKE

This camp on Shackelton Point was closer to the point itself. It was a very peaceful and relaxing atmosphere. However, when the steamboat came in, there was also much partying. (Courtesy of Carol Greene.)

After Charles Shackelton's death in 1895, the property was sold to Alexander T. Brown, who had over 300 patents for his inventions. One of his sons, Charles S. Brown, purchased some property in 1928. Then, after his father's death, he bought out his brother's share of the property and began building. Seen here is a clubhouse for gambling and other activities. Next to that building was a six-car garage where dances were held. (Courtesy of Cornell University Biological Field Station.)

Charles Brown added buildings and remodeled some existing farm buildings. However, he never did any farming. He did have a kennel for his famous Great Danes. People would see them when they were taken out for car rides by their handler. There were also many gazebos, a library, a maple sugar shack, and several other buildings. (Courtesy of Cornell University Biological Field Station.)

This was Charles Brown's home. It was located on Shackelton Point, very close to the lake. Many guests were invited to parties held at the house. The style of the home goes along with his plans to build a "Little Williamsburg" at the point. There was also other housing for his extensive staff. Most of the buildings from Brown's estate have been well preserved and still exist today. (Courtesy of Cornell University Biological Field Station.)

This photograph shows some of the many buildings on the estate, as well as the point. Paul Laible worked for Charles Brown as the site superintendent. Laible planted many trees on the estate, including the evergreens seen here. Many of these trees are fully grown today. (Courtesy of Cornell University Biological Field Station.)

Upon Charles Brown's death, he left his estate at Shackelton's Point to Cornell University. He had graduated from Cornell and was also very interested in science. Brown had patents for his many inventions. The property is now known as the Cornell University Biological Field Station. This image shows one of the boats used by Cornell students in the summer, when they do research on the scientific changes occurring in the waters and fish life in Oneida Lake. (Courtesy of Cornell University Biological Field Station.)

This camp is southwest of the Cornell estate on Briggs Bay. The bay is just behind Dutchman's Island. The camp was owned by the Lucas family and built in 1939. Caroline Lucas lived here and married Paul Laible, who worked for Cornell and for Charles Brown when he owned the estate. (Courtesy of Charles Laible.)

This monument was erected by the Syracuse Chapter of the Sons of the American Revolution and the State of New York in 1930. It is located on Bridgeport-Kirkville Road, on what used to be the Abraham and Flora Bitz farm. A stockade fort was built in 1756 along Chittenango Creek, behind the farms and present buildings, for the protection of the Tuscarora tribe. In 1780, during a battle here, 50 men were tortured under a tree, which is referred to as the Turtle Tree and is still remembered today. A short distance north of here, there is a place in the creek where the Indians built a wall of boulders. In the summer, they stored fish behind the wall until they had time to dry them for winter use. The wall is still partially there today.

Five

ONEIDA LAKE
ACTIVITIES AND SCENERY

Robert Porter is seen here in the early 1940s on Billington Bay in a sailboat he built himself. Harmon C. Landgraff writes in *Oneida Lake, Past and Present* that "Oneida Lake's general effect is one of great but quiet beauty. To those who live on its banks for any length of time, seeing and knowing its various moods and phases in calm and storm, observing day after day its ever-changing hues of sky and water and its shifting wonders of clouds, and looking out on its splendid sunsets, when the low-lying clouds on the western horizon are made crimson and golden and cast a vast halo of light and color and glory over the western sky, it is beautiful beyond description. The delicate shades and tints, the tracings of water and sky so glowing, so ethereal, so altogether lovely, cannot be surpassed, its friends and lovers believe." (Courtesy of Virginia Porter.)

In the late 1800s, steamboats traveled on Oneida Lake. It was a great way to cruise along and cool off on a summer day. Along the way, there were scheduled stops at hotels and restaurants on the shore. This photograph appears to show Fisher Bay, with Damon Point on the left side.

This rowboat ride also took place in Fisher Bay. The buildings of the Fisher farm are clearly visible on the far shore. Susan Langley, an expert on historical clothing styles, believes this was taken in the 1870s. Note the chairs in the boat, rather than just a built-in board to sit on.

The group of ladies in the background appears to have just stepped ashore from their boats, on the west side of Shackelton Point. It would not have been easy to get in and out of the boats, as there is no dock in the area, and the ladies' long dresses were likely cumbersome. This area was near where there had been camps at one time. (Courtesy of Carol Greene.)

A group of younger boaters explores the lake in a craft that is just the right size for them. This photograph was taken in Briggs Bay, with Shackelton Point in the background, in September 1947. The boy pulling the duck decoys is James Laible, and the boy on the far right is Charles Laible. Their grandfather Lucas is in the boat behind them. (Courtesy of Charles Laible.)

Jackie Barrett and his father, Conrad, get ready to go for a ride in their speedboat in Fisher Bay in the late 1930s. Behind them are their farmhouse and another camp. Note that young Jackie is not wearing a life jacket, as it was a different era.

Seen here is the very beginning of the excavation for Fisher Bay Marina. There had always been a small stream there that came in from Oneida Lake. The stream was deepened and widened to accommodate boats. The two men checking out the progress are Burdette MacAdam (right) and Conrad Barrett, the first owners of the marina. This first digging occurred in 1953. (Courtesy of William Barrett.)

Fisher Bay Marina is seen here in 1960, after the channel and two ponds had been dug. To the right is the metal shed where boats were stored in the winter. Many docks were put in to secure the boats. The little shed on the channel was the office, and there was a dock to buy gas. In 2006, the marina was sold to a housing developer, and houses are being built around the ponds in 2014. The purchasers of the houses have docks right out their front doors to go out to their boats. (Courtesy of William Barrett.)

In 1905, construction was begun on the Barge Canal System. The original Erie Canal did not go through Oneida Lake. A lot of changes have been made, however, and now the canal system can take one from Oneida Lake to Albany or to Buffalo. Many locks were constructed to accomplish this. This photograph shows the barges that tugboats moved through the canal system. These barges were kept at Sylvan Beach during the winter. There are no more barges today, but the canal system is still open for pleasure craft as part of the New York State Canal System. (Courtesy of Daniel Ward, PhD, Erie Canal Museum, Syracuse.)

There are frequently absolutely gorgeous sunsets on Oneida Lake. As the sun goes down, the colors are reflected on the water, and the sky around the sun turns many shades of orange. Seen here in front of the sunset is a bass boat. Bass fishing has become very important, and there are even bass fishing tournaments held on the lake now, with fishermen coming great distances to compete for large prizes. (Courtesy of Kate Anyon, Chasing Sunsets Photography.)

For many years, beautiful swans have stopped to visit Oneida Lake. They are often spotted on Fisher Bay, but they move around to other spots on the lake at different times. While traveling from lakes to the north, they stop over on Oneida Lake for a while. Then, as soon as the lake freezes, they continue south. While there are only six swans in this photograph, numbers as high as the 70s have been counted. Note the swan on the right with its head down in the water, probably feeding on weeds from the bottom of the lake.

Swimsuits have certainly changed over the years. These bathers cool off in the refreshing water of Oneida Lake. Many spots along the lake have sand and a gradual increase in water depth. Sometimes, people prefer to go out in their boats so they can dive into deeper water. (Courtesy of Jean Prawl.)

The Town of Sullivan Parks and Recreation Department is in charge of Chapman Park. It is located on Route 31 just east of Bridgeport and includes well-maintained facilities. There is a beach, a fishing pier, soccer, softball and baseball fields, tennis and basketball courts, a play yard for kids, and pavilions to use for picnics and parties. For several weeks, there are live band performances one night of the week. People have to sign up early to reserve pavilions for parties and family reunions.

In the late 1940s or early 1950s, Leroy "Cub" Sternberg created what was likely the first snowmobile in the area. He used an airplane engine and propeller to make it run. It was much larger than today's machines and had little protection from the wind. Sternberg would head down North Road from Bridgeport and out onto the lake to go ice fishing. People still fish on the lake, but many now use four-wheelers and drag a little fish house behind them. (Courtesy of Deb Honors.)

Instead of a famous Damon boat, this is a famous Damon iceboat. This was invented by Loren and Ceylon Damon in the late 1920s. Ceylon is seen here with two of his children, Ronald and Irma. With a good wind, the iceboat could really move along. The wide skis must have made it possible to stay on top of the snow. (Courtesy of Karen Miller.)

Bombardier Ski-Doo came out with its first snowmobile sleds in 1959. This have always been a popular brand in this area. They can go across fields and, if the ice is thick enough, travel on the lake. Sometimes in the winter, the lake looks like a busy street of headlights. Here, Jeffrey (right) and John Barrett run their own sleds, wearing snowmobile suits, boots, gloves, and helmets. (Courtesy of William Barrett.)

Sometimes in spring, the lake can be dangerous for people on the ice, as well as houses close to shore. When the ice starts to break up, the wind can make it come crashing up on shore and damage camps and homes, as happened here. If fishermen are on the lake as it breaks up, they can get trapped on a floating piece of ice and need to be rescued.

Six

FARMS

In 1915, a Grange was organized in Bridgeport. With the number of farms in the area, it was well attended and supported. A building on Route 31 was purchased for the Grange to hold meetings. In later years, after the new school was constructed, the Grange met in the old school building. This photograph shows a Grange picnic at a local farm in July 1921.

The Grange picnic was held at a local farm with tables and chairs set up on the lawn by the farmhouse. The farmers' wives were surely happy to bring and share their favorite foods.

Along the shore of Oneida Lake was the Fisher farm. It was made up of property bought from several smaller farms in the late 1800s. The property was then inherited by Fisher's daughter, Florence Barrett. In the early days, the work on the farm was done by many hired hands. The farmhouse is seen here.

In later years, Florence Barrett's son and grandsons owned it and did much of the farmwork. It was a dairy farm with Holstein cows. In the early years, raw milk was bottled and sold by the Barretts. Later, the milk was sold to the Dairymen's League in Syracuse. The Barretts also picked up milk from other farms to take to Syracuse. The farm's barns are seen here.

This photograph gives an idea of how deep snow can get in the area. This was taken during the 1940 blizzard. The road had been plowed, but only for one lane of traffic. When similar conditions occurred in earlier years, horses and sleighs were used to get to Bridgeport.

In the early days at the Fisher farm, trees and branches were sawed and the wood was stockpiled in the basement of the house for heat in the winter. In later years, coal was used. The house had one opening from the furnace, in the living room. If one went upstairs or to the kitchen, it was very cold.

At the Fisher farm in the early days, there were many horse-drawn wagons and vehicles to go to town or for when people came to visit. There was a hitching post and stairs for people to get out of their buggies in front of the farmhouse (left). There also were not any electric lines along the dirt road. In those days, different types of lanterns were used for light in the house and the barn. At the end of the road, there was a hill and a cow pasture down to the lake. The second door on the barn opened to a dirt hill going down into the cow barns that were under the hay barns.

Conrad Fisher was a gentleman farmer. He probably did little of the farmwork himself. There were hired hands to do the milking, crop harvesting, and other chores. He and his wife, Louisa, had a home in Minoa and used the lake mainly as a summer home.

This farm, on Damon's Point, was originally run by Norton Damon. Later, his grandson Leon ran the farm. When Leon was young, he worked for his father, Loren Damon, at the Damon boat factory in town. Leon married Blondelia Collar, and they ran this operation mostly as a dairy farm. Leon eventually began to lease lots for people to build summer camps along the lakeshore on Oneida Lake. (Courtesy of Raymond and Joyce Damon.)

This image shows farmers filling their hay wagon to take hay to the barns for storage. All of this work was done by hand. The hay was cut, raked, and loaded on the wagon, and then, when they got back to the barn, it was thrown by hand into the haymow. (Courtesy of Barbara Niederhoff.)

Etherbert Whitman owned this farm along Route 31. It is seen here during the worst years of the Depression. In the 1930s, the family had a farm stand along Route 31 run by Jessie Karker Whitman, the wife of Hudson Whitman. She sold vegetables grown on the farm. The house has been updated and still stands on Route 31 as part of the Rogues' Roost Golf & Country Club. (Courtesy of Dawn Seeber.)

The treadle sewing machine, operated by a foot pedal, was invented in the United States in the 1800s. There were several companies seeking patents in the 1850s, including Singer. This model is not a Singer. Some people still use the treadle machine to sew heavy materials like canvas. The needles on these machines do not break as easily as on newer electric machines. (Courtesy of Dawn Seeber.)

Rogues' Roost Golf & Country Club opened in 1964. The property was made up of acreage bought from several farmers in the area. The clubhouse was a converted former barn from Fred and Bertha Gifford's farm. This image shows the back of the building, right where golfers tee off for the West Course. On the front of the building, facing Route 31, is an unusual logo. It represents a rogue "Pirate" who, legend says, lived on a high spot in the middle of the Cicero Swamp. He would come out of the swamp at night and rob the locals. The logo is a golf ball with a black eye patch and a curling black mustache. (Courtesy of Darl Johnston.)

The Gifford farm was located on the south side of Route 31. The house in the center belonged to Fred and Bertha Gifford. Their son Carl lived in the home on the left with his wife and three sons. After Fred passed away, the family stopped farming. Carl sold International Harvester tractors and also repaired tractors in the barn, as seen here. The barn behind this building later became the Rogues' Roost clubhouse. (Courtesy of Darl Johnston.)

This used to be a tenant house on the Robert Barr Sr. farm on Smithridge Road. The farmhouse and barn were quite a distance from it. In recent times, the farm was owned by Fred and Jean Jackson. It is no longer a farm, and there are now six homes, each on a very large lot, between the farm and the tenant house. (Courtesy of Dawn Seeber.)

Billington's Bay Farm was owned by Pharon J. and Maude M. Billington. The house and barn were on Shackelton Point Road. Today, they are separated by the road. The property extended to Oneida Lake and along the shore for a very long distance. Today, this house is surrounded by many newer homes. These were once camps, but, over the years, they have been converted into beautiful year-round residences. (Courtesy of Carol Greene.)

The Jackson house (above) and barn (below) have been located on Smithridge Road in Bridgeport since around 1910. The present owners, Dennis and Carol Rider, shared their deed with the author, and that is the first date on it. It is referred to as the Jackson farm here because the Jacksons did the major repairs to the house and barn in 1940. Around 1926, a tornado damaged the chicken house and took the roof off the barn. The barn roof was replaced with a hip roof, and a new chicken house was built. Today, the Riders have started raising chickens, and they are very interested in preserving the house and the barn. (Both, courtesy of Dennis and Carol Rider.)

The Hubert Ladd farm on Route 31 began as a dairy farm. Today's Ladd Road was originally part of the farm fields. In later years, when the family stopped farming the land, they rented out their fields to other farmers for hay. The house still stands today. (Courtesy of Dawn Seeber.)

Jim Bailey (driving) and Barney LaGrange are seen here on a motorcycle in 1942. Route 31 is in the distance behind them. There are no trees in the fields at this time. Bailey had come to visit and to take LaGrange for a ride. The motorcycle is parked next to the LaGrange farm on Petrie Road. (Courtesy of Jim Bailey.)

The Barney and Aggie LaGrange chicken farm was on Petrie Road. The farmhouse has had some remodeling over the years and is presently owned by Donald and Carol Colella. (Courtesy of Don and Carol Colella.)

This farm was once owned by the Ostrowski family. Before that, a very early owner, a Mr. Rector, supposedly allowed Native Americans to cure and store fish in his barn. Chittenango Creek is right behind the barn. They were using the creek and lake as a source of food for the winter months. Another former owner was Thomas Sleeth. At one point, a fire caused by spontaneous combustion totally destroyed the barn. Fortunately, the recently built home was saved. (Courtesy of Donna Egan.)

The Sayles farm is seen here in the 1920s. Through marriage, it later became the Leaman farm. In those days, farmers depended on horses to pull the wagons and other farm equipment. The hay was cut by hand with a scythe and then loaded on wagons with pitchforks. Farms also usually had a few cows, chickens, horses, and vegetable gardens. (Courtesy of Barbara Block.)

Grant Sayles is seen here taking target practice next to the outhouse. The fields from the farm went all the way to Oneida Lake, where the family had a camp for summer use. They could catch fish and shoot ducks and other animals to use for food. (Courtesy of Barbara Block.)

Roy Leaman is seen at left with his mother and an unidentified soldier friend in 1922. Roy had been in World War I. The woman below is Helen Sayles. She and her husband, Llewyn, ran a cheese factory down the road. When it began to fail, they moved to this Leaman house, where they started a small farm to grow food that helped them survive the Depression. Sayles was the grandmother of Barbara Block, who shared these photographs. (Both, courtesy of Barbara Block.)

Joseph Pindle II is seen here in his buggy with his two sons, Frank (left) and Ed. The horse is named Jimmy. Judging by the sons' ages, the photograph was taken around 1910. They are on their way to the Catholic church in Minoa, six miles away. The farmhouse seen here burned in 1946. Very sadly, Joseph's wife, Rose, was lost in the fire. (Courtesy of William Pindle.)

This painting, entitled *Original Pindle Homestead*, is by local artist Donna Egan. This was the home of Joseph II and Rose Pindle. The farm was located on the Bridgeport-Kirkville Road on the hill about a mile south of Route 31. (Courtesy of Donna Egan.)

CASE
Horse Drawn
DISK HARROW

Sold By
FRANK M. PINDLE
Bridgeport, N.Y.

Farm machinery
Dealer 1928-1940

J. I. CASE CO. INC.
ESTABLISHED 1842
RACINE, WISCONSIN · U.S.A.

This is the Pindle barn that was on the hill just outside of Bridgeport. At the time this photograph was taken, the barn was used by Ed and Frank Pindle as part of their farm. Ed lived just down the road in a house that had another dairy barn. Frank lived on Route 31 with his family, but he helped out on the farm. Frank also had a building next to his Route 31 house where he worked as a dealer of Case Horse Drawn Disk Harrows (left). He was a farm machinery dealer from 1920 to 1940. (Both, courtesy of William Pindle.)

The original Pindle farm was on Pindle Lane, which goes from Shackelton Point Road down to Oneida Lake. The first owners were Joseph I and Walburger Pindle. They had nine children. Joseph Pindle II was the last to live on Pindle Lane. Much later, that property was bought by Cornell University. The house was moved to Petrie Road and the buildings still left were destroyed. The house is now owned by Harry and Ann Hale. (Courtesy of Raymond and Joyce Damon.)

This 1950 aerial photograph shows the John and Lottie Beilic home, which was on the west side of Chittenango Creek along Route 31, bordering the Elton Roberts dairy farm. The second house belonged to Roberts's son Glenn. (Courtesy of Jeanne Roberts Brown.)

In this photograph, of the area across Route 31 from that in the image on the previous page, are the barns of the Elton Roberts dairy farm, which were later lost in a fire. They were located near Route 31's present-day entrance to Val Park and Oneida Park. A young Jeanne Roberts is playing in the grass with her grandmother Beulah Grant in 1947. Chittenango Creek runs not far behind most of the Roberts buildings on the north side of Route 31. (Courtesy of Jeanne Roberts Brown.)

Farther down Route 31 were this schoolhouse and Elton Roberts's home (left). The house was first owned by Elton's father, Jesse. It no longer stands, but the school does. Glenn Roberts was an insurance salesman who worked out of his home for years. The school was put up for auction after it was closed in the 1950s. Eventually, Elton acquired it. Glenn then moved his insurance business into the former school. Later, Jeanne Roberts Brown, Glenn's daughter, opened a beauty shop in the building. After that, Dick Roberts, Jeanne's brother, remodeled the outside of the schoolhouse to look as it first did. It even has a bell on the roof, as it did in the old days. Dick's family now lives there. (Courtesy of Jeanne Roberts Brown.)

Farther down Route 31 are more of Elton Roberts's farm barns. They were located right across from the turn onto Bull Road. When the Roberts family stopped farming, Elton began hauling dirt and stone for people. (Courtesy of Jeanne Roberts Brown.)

The Russell farm was located on the corner of Routes 31 and 298. Paul and Pearl Russell purchased the farm from Thomas Sleeth around 1941. There is a Sunoco gas station there now, and the former farm field across the road is now full of businesses and the Val Park and Oneida Park home development. There is also a senior citizen apartment complex, as well as St. Francis Catholic Church. The fenced-in area in the lower right corner is quicksand, only a mile or so from Cicero Swamp. The farmers fenced it in to keep out the cows. (Courtesy of Bonnie Dean Gallauresi.)

The Donald and Hilda Sayles farm still stands today on Bull Road in Bridgeport. The dairy farm was there as early as 1921. Donald had two brothers, Oney and Stuart Sayles. Bull Road was still a dirt road when this photograph was taken. The buildings were well constructed; even though the farm is no longer operational, the house and barn are in good condition. (Courtesy of Caroline Wichie Van Allen.)

Floyd Palmer is seen here with dogs Barney and Sport in a Ford Model T that belonged to his father, Newton. Floyd was never a farmer, but he had a camp on Hitchcock Point. His brother Frank had a farm on Route 31 across from Tuttle Road. (Courtesy of Jean Prawl.)

Newton Palmer owned a farm on Route 31 very close to Tyler Road. This photograph shows his barn and him feeding his geese. The farmhouse still stands today, but the barns are gone. There is now a street called Palmer Drive off of Tyler Road. Palmer had a camp on Oneida Lake; later, more camps were built there on Palmer Drive. Today, those former camps are year-round homes. (Courtesy of Jean Prawl.)

BRIDGEPORT CHEESE FACTORY.

ACCOUNT SALES _Aug 31_ _____ 188_3_

To _J McChie_ _____ Patron.

Sale No. _12_ No. of Cheese sold _108_ Weighing _6434_ lbs. Price sold for _9¾_ cts. per lb. Amount of Sale, $ _627.31_ Comprising Cheese from _Aug 6_ to _15_ both days included. Whole No. lbs. Milk _66638_ No. lbs. Milk required for 1 lb. Cheese _10 3/_ Your share Milk _2254_ lbs. $ _____ Amount due you, $1.35 per 100 lbs., for making, &c., deducted, $ _18.17_

This receipt from a cheese factory in Cicero is dated August 31, 1883. The receipt is one of a whole stack of receipts kept through the years. Farmers quite often sold milk directly to cheese factories to increase their income. John Wichie was the patron. (Courtesy of Thomas Mafrici.)

The Wichie farmhouse, first operated by John Wichie in the 1880s, still stands today on Bull Road in Bridgeport. Wichie's son Irving and grandson Carroll continued the operation of the farm until Carroll retired from farming in 1970. (Courtesy of Carolyn Wichie Van Allen.)

The Wright farm was located on North Road. The property is no longer a farm, but the house and barn are still there. Walter and Jenny Wright were the owners at one time. It is said the house was moved from the property of its original owner, Alvin Sternberg, to the farm location. The Wrights' daughter, Betty, married Robert Tubbert, and they lived in a house directly across from the farm on North Road. (Courtesy of Cyndy Brancato.)

UNITED STATES
OF AMERICA
War Ration Book One

WARNING

1 Punishments ranging as high as *Ten Years' Imprisonment or $10,000 Fine, or Both*, may be imposed under United States Statutes for violations thereof arising out of infractions of Rationing Orders and Regulations.

2 This book must not be transferred. It must be held and used only by or on behalf of the person to whom it has been issued, and anyone presenting it thereby represents to the Office of Price Administration, an agency of the United States Government, that it is being so held and so used. For any misuse of this book it may be taken from the holder by the Office of Price Administration.

3 In the event either of the departure from the United States of the person to whom this book is issued, or his or her death, the book must be surrendered in accordance with the Regulations.

4 Any person finding a lost book must deliver it promptly to the nearest Ration Board.

N?. 815199 –313

OFFICE OF PRICE ADMINISTRATION

The date for this war ration book is 1942. Many things in stores were rationed, which meant one was only allowed to purchase a certain amount of the product. Commonly rationed products were sugar, butter, and gasoline. The books dictated how much one was allowed to buy so that products could be distributed equally among the population. (Courtesy of Dawn Seeber.)

In 1923, Stewart Herman sold some of his farm property and this house to his son Lewis for $1. They both continued working on the farm for some time. The two Herman farmhouses were across the road from each other. They are still there along the Bridgeport-Kirkville Road. (Courtesy of Phil and Donna McCarten.)

Stewart Herman's home is seen here in the 1930s. The house was originally built in 1896 by siblings William and Frances Johnston. It changed hands several times before Herman bought it in 1917. (Courtesy of Esther Goodell.)

In the late 1800s, a family from New York City built a summer home that later became the Cramer Crouch farmhouse. The wood used to construct the house was hemlock. It was shipped on the Erie Canal, which went through Kirkville, just up the road from the house. Cramer and Norma Crouch were the last ones to run the farm. Their daughter Lynn remembers that one could climb stairs all the way to the cupola on top of the house. (Courtesy of Donna Egan.)

The last people to buy the former Crouch house planned to refurbish it but ran out of money, opting instead to burn the house, as seen here. Some people say that the house was haunted and they can see ghosts' faces in the smoke pictured here. (Courtesy of Deb Honors.)

Seven

ALONG BRIDGEPORT ROADS

This aerial photograph shows a much-changed Bridgeport. The creek is still there, as well as several of the original homes and buildings from the 1800s. However, what was mostly farmland on the Cicero side of the bridge became a shopping area and a housing development called Val Park and Oneida Park in the early 1960s. Only one farm's buildings can be seen, but it was no longer operating. (Courtesy of Thomas Mafrici.)

The Gothic house usually referred to as "the Gingerbread House" by the locals of Bridgeport was built by Henry W. Gifford. Alice Kneeskern and her husband, Irwin "Sam," lived in the house and ran Greentree Nursery in back of it. Alice was also an elementary school teacher. (Courtesy of Caroline Nojaim.)

In 1937, a tractor-trailer truck jackknifed and crashed into the front of the house belonging to Frank Pindle and his family, on Route 31 just east of the bridge. This sort of thing often happened at the intersection of Routes 31 and 298, on the west side of the bridge. At that intersection, there is a sharp curve. The goods being carried often spilled all over the road. If it were a type of canned goods, for example, people would come running to pick up the spilled products. (Courtesy of Dawn Pindle Falge.)

Both of these houses were east of the businesses on Route 31. The house above was built in 1903. The Coleman family bought it from Bertha Gifford in the spring of 1937. Later, Jeannette Coleman Bush and her family lived there. Today, it has been turned into a beauty shop. The Frank Bryant Sr. house is seen at right. Bryant's wife, Julia, is on the roof of the porch painting the house. At the time, there was a chicken coop in the backyard. Many of the Bryant children still live in the area today. (Above, courtesy of Jeannette Coleman Bush; right, courtesy of Frank Bryant.)

This house on North Road was originally owned by Lottie Brown Fox, the sister of Dick and David Brown. In later times, the home belonged to Carl and Esther Goodell. They were married in 1946 and had four children. Esther now lives in what was the Herman farmhouse on Bridgeport-Kirkville Road. (Courtesy of Esther Goodell.)

Ida Groesbeck stands on the porch of her home on North Road. She is Irene Sternberg's grandmother. Younger relatives remember that she always had homemade cookies in her cookie jar when they came to visit. This house, now owned by a different family, still stands today. (Courtesy of Deb Honors.)

This is an old, undated photograph of the David and Rose Brown house. The two ladies sitting in front of the porch are David Brown's sister Leah Brown Collar and their mother, Blondelia Brown. (Courtesy of Raymond and Joyce Damon.)

This house, on Route 31 next to Dick Brown's house, was known as the Gifford house. The lady and her gentleman caller are unidentified, but this photograph was certainly taken at an early time, as he is traveling in a horse-drawn vehicle. Their clothing is also likely from the late 1800s. Bertha Gifford, whose husband owned a farm east of Bridgeport, came to live at this house after her husband passed. (Courtesy of Carol Greene.)

The view in this photograph looks east on Route 31 at the D.H. Brown store (left). To the right of the store is the home of David and Rose Brown. Past that is the home of David's brother Dick and his wife, Ella. Note that there are electric lines by this time and that the big porch on David's house is no longer there. (Courtesy of Carol Greene.)

Comparing this to the photograph at the top of the page shows that the houses are seen here at a much earlier time. David Brown's porch is still there, there is a hitching post in front of the house, and Route 31 is not yet paved. The third house down is the Gifford home. All three homes still stand today on Route 31. (Courtesy of Carol Greene.)

This cobblestone house is on the corner of Route 31 and Smithridge Road. This photograph does not show the big front porch that was originally on the house. Karen Miller (a Damon relative) said that, at one time, the house had a porch that went all the way around the structure. Her father told her how he used to roller-skate all around the porch. The double window in the center of the first floor was once a set of double doors. The home was built by Edmond Damon, who was born in 1809 and started building the house when he was about 18. The stones were hauled from Oneida Lake with the help of his sisters. He married Sarah Hicks in 1835, and they moved into the residence. In 1861, he and his family moved to Iowa. The house was later a tavern and then the home for the Carter farm.

In October 1954, Hurricane Hazel came through Bridgeport. Many trees fell and houses were damaged. This photograph shows the Dan Harwood home on Bridgeport-Kirkville Road. (Courtesy of Dawn Pindle Falge.)

This has often been the scene on Route 298 going out of Bridgeport. Heavy rains or fast snowmelts cause the road to flood. The road goes through Cicero Swamp, so the drainage is not good. When the roadway was first built, crews installed train tracks to haul in the needed materials. There is a story told that when the men came to work one morning the tracks and the train on it were gone. There is quicksand in the swamp. (Courtesy of Barbara Block.)

This is a sad photograph of a terrible accident. Joe Pindle was flying his Waco plane in 1926 when he crashed in a field near Routes 31 and 298, close to the future entrance to Oneida Park and Val Park. He was killed in the crash. He and Frank Pindle used to land the plane on their airstrip, in a field where Blanding's Hardware is now located. (Courtesy of William Pindle.)

Eight

PLACES PEOPLE GATHER

In 1835, a Methodist Episcopal Society was formed in Bridgeport. At first, it met in members' homes. Then it met in a former Baptist church. Soon, members decided to build their own church. It was constructed with timber from the area and pegs made in the village. The first service in the new church was held on March 18, 1869. In the next 55 years, the church had 29 pastors. Many boxed-lunch fundraisers were held over the years to support the ministers. In 1886, a parsonage was built next to the church. (Courtesy of Dawn Seeber.)

In 1943, the church became known as the Bridgeport Methodist Church. The year 1945 was a bad one for the church, as fire destroyed the original building. Arrangements were made to let the members of the church use the second floor of the fire hall until a new church could be built. The long fundraising effort began, and, in 1950, members held the first service in their new church, on the corner of Route 31 and North Road. (Courtesy of Marilyn Simmons.)

Rev. Baden Mudge was the minister at the Bridgeport Methodist Church for 37 years—1926 to 1963. At the same time, he served as a minister for the Methodist churches in Cicero Center and, at various times, in Lakeport. In the 1940s, he did a weekly 15-minute talk on radio station WOLF in Syracuse called *Down Rural Lanes*. The object of the talk was to bring city and country people to a better understanding of each other's problems. To say the least, he was a much-loved member of the hamlet of Bridgeport. (Courtesy of Bridgeport Methodist Church.)

Over the years, the Methodist church has made several changes to its building. A stained-glass window was installed, and a very large addition built behind the church included a kitchen and a dining room for dinners. Also, several classrooms were built for Sunday school. In the 1980s, these rooms were used for an Ecumenical Bible School for the Methodist church and St. Francis Catholic Church. Thanks to the many volunteers from both churches, it was a huge success.

For many years, Catholics in Bridgeport traveled to Minoa for mass. In 1947, a priest from Minoa began to come to Bridgeport to say mass upstairs in the fire hall. Because of the great attendance, a Catholic church was eventually established in Bridgeport. The church was built in 1951, and the same order of Franciscan priests that served in Minoa appointed a priest for the new parish. The church was named for St. Francis of Assisi. Until a rectory was built for the priest to live in, he lived in the basement of the church. More recently, a parish center was constructed next to the church, with classrooms and facilities for holding mass and social events. (Courtesy of Ed Karl.)

For years, Bridgeport had this two-room schoolhouse, where grades one through eight were taught. Until centralization in the 1950s, those going on to high school traveled to Minoa. Teachers usually went through a two-year normal school program to prepare for the job. Before these training schools existed, it was usually someone who could read and write that taught. A bell on top of the school was rung at the beginning of the day. Every Halloween, some of the local boys would climb the roof and take the bell. It was always found and put back. (Courtesy of Carol Greene.)

These pieces of school memorabilia were actually used by teachers and students at the Bridgeport school. The desk and stool were used by R.O. Cook, who came to Bridgeport around 1876, at the age of 16, to be a teacher. The globe, the inkwell with the feather, and flag are from that school. They were salvaged from the attic of the building before it was torn down. (Courtesy of Duane Schiebler.)

More memorabilia from the Bridgeport school is seen here, including another globe, a bell to let the children know recess was over, a rolled map, and sticks used to point things out on the map. These books were actually used by students long ago. The desks were usually hooked together, so each desk was attached to the seat of the student in front. The desks were also not movable, as they were attached to the floor. (Courtesy of Duane Schiebler.)

IN MEMORY OF

HIRAM AND BETSY HUBBARD

WHO DONATED THIS PROPERTY
IN 1868 FOR
THE EDUCATION OF AREA
YOUTH

REDONATED TO THE TOWN OF
SULLIVAN BY THEIR GREAT
GREAT GRANDCHILDREN

ARLINE H. BROWN
MARVIN W. HUBBARD
JOHN C. HUBBARD

This marker is located on the side of Chapman Park. It marks the spot where another one-room school existed. The foundation of that building is still there. When the property was donated to the Town of Sullivan, it was turned over to the parks and recreation department, which helped set up the park and still runs it today.

Seen at right is Lois Long (now Parsons), who taught at this one-room school in the early 1940s. It was located right across from the end of Smithridge Road on Route 31. This school was one mile from the two-room school in the center of Bridgeport. The schools were set up that way so that students did not have to walk too far to get to a school building. Long is ringing the bell to let the children know that school is starting. She recalls that she boarded at a farmhouse across the road from the school. All unwed teachers were required to board with a family in the area. Her duties as a teacher included getting to school early each morning to get the fire started and bring in drinking water for the children. The same school is seen below in 1919 with students posing for a class picture in front of it. The students are a variety of ages, as there was only one teacher, a Miss Gregg. Some of the students are, in no particular order, Irene Barr, Harlow Roberts, Lora Carter, and Uretta Myers. (Both, courtesy of Dawn Seeber.)

This 1920s photograph shows students who attended the Bridgeport two-room schoolhouse, including Frank Pindle (middle row, far right). The school had one teacher in each room. The home in the background, on North Road, was later owned by Esther Goodell. (Courtesy of Dawn Pindle Falge.)

These students appear to be nearly old enough to go on to high school in Minoa. The photograph is dated around 1925. It is difficult to tell the difference between students and teachers in the standing rows. Two of the seated students are Conrad Barrett (fourth from left) and William Brown (third from right).

The interior of one of the two rooms in the Bridgeport schoolhouse is seen here. This class includes students in grades one through eight. With only one teacher, students of similar ages were often put together, and many older students helped teach younger ones. (Courtesy of Karen Miller.)

This is an unusual composite image of individual student photographs, along with that of their teacher, from the Bridgeport school's class of 1939. Pictured are, from left to right, (top row) Mary Wuiliem, Shirley Jardine, Nancy Mudge, Nona Bitz, Vidal Wuiliez, Charles Huffman, Midge Sternberg, and Janice Backenstross; (second row) Janette Coleman, Pudgy DeVore, Gene Damon, Barbara Lum, Shirley Bitz, Alan Wilcox, Mae Burlingame, Herman Sternberg, and Dick Lee; (third row) Leona Sandro, Russ Groesbeck, Janette Dean, Rita Deyo, Alice Wilcox, Paul Damon, Barb Kneeskern, Merritt Roberts, and Dale Huffman; (fourth row) Martha Coleman, Lillian Harp, Alfred Lee, Jean Robinson, Prof. Paul Taylor, Kent Dodge, Geraldine Lee, Gary LaGrange, and Gordon Lum; (bottom row) Bernie Costello, Marilyn Lum, Lois Coleman, Marleah Roberts, Anson Burlingame, Vic Dean, Mary Louis Goodell, Nancy Kneeskern, and Joy Damon. (Courtesy of Karen Miller.)

In 1947, classes had become far too large for the two-room schoolhouse in Bridgeport. This photograph shows students in kindergarten through second grade. These classes were held in the building next to the Bridgeport Playhouse that later became Miller Hardware. Flora Bitz taught all three grades.

The Bridgeport Mother's Club created this float for the fire company parade. This was in the late 1940s or early 1950s, when the centralization of the Bridgeport and Chittenango schools was being discussed. Patricia Fox is the baton twirler. (Courtesy of Patricia Hogan.)

The new Bridgeport School opened in 1952 as part of the Chittenango Central School System. An addition was built in later years. At this time, it held kindergarten through sixth grade. In the top left corner is the former farm of Clark Damon on Shackelton Point Road. (Courtesy of Karen Miller.)

In the new school, Caroline Laible was a kindergarten teacher. Finally, all grades from kindergarten through sixth were taught in the same building in Bridgeport. Also, each class had its own enclosed classroom. Laible had been a very active member of the Bridgeport Mother's Club. This group of women did much to help make this happen. (Courtesy of Charles Laible.)

After many years of planning, a Veterans of Foreign Wars (VFW) post was opened in Bridgeport. It is located on Route 31. At the base of the Bridgeport side of the monument are bricks with soldiers' names engraved on them. The VFW building can be rented for weddings, graduation parties, and many other occasions.

This building was located next to the firehouse on Route 31. At one time, Don Moyer ran a barbershop here. Later, it became the location of the Bridgeport Library. It was later joined with the Chittenango Library to become the Town of Sullivan Library. The Bridgeport Mother's Club had a hand in getting this first library started. (Courtesy of Dawn Pindle Falge.)

This is the newer library in Bridgeport, located on North Road. It opened in 1973. This library and 42 other public libraries in Herkimer, Madison, and Oneida Counties are members of the Mid York Library System. Plans are currently being made to build an addition onto this library. (Courtesy of Karen Fauls Traynor.)

The Bridgeport Volunteer Fire Department has been expertly servicing the area since 1935. This photograph shows just a few of the many different vehicles that have been used over the years. In addition to fighting fires, the department also helps out at the scenes of automobile accidents, as well as rescues on Oneida Lake. It has a boat for that purpose. (Courtesy of William Pindle.)

The original fire company building was constructed around 1935. Many groups have held meetings here. The Methodist and Catholic churches used the upstairs room for services when their own church buildings were not available. Seen through the right garage door is the first school bus for Bridgeport, which was stored there when not in use. (Courtesy of William Pindle.)

IN MEMORY OF
THE MEMBERS OF THE
BRIDGEPORT FIRE DEPT.
AND LADIES AUXILIARY
WHO HAVE DEDICATED
THEIR SERVICES
TO THE COMMUNITY

In recent years, the Bridgeport Fire Department added this monument next to the fire building. No names are listed on it, but it recognizes all the members of the fire department and the ladies auxiliary for their service to the community. Over the years, this has included quite a lot of people.

Parades down Route 31 have always been held in the summer, including Fourth of July parades, as seen here. Note the bands and soldiers marching and the vintage cars along the road. At the top of the image is the D.H. Brown store. (Courtesy of Raymond and Joyce Damon.)

This float was an entry in the 1954 firemen's parade. These parades have been held for many years over Labor Day weekend. Here, girls from Bridgeport competed to be the princess of the village. The princess (seated) and her court waved to the crowds. In the background, between the granary building and the Esso station, is a diner. (Courtesy of Dawn Pindle Falge.)

This is another Fourth of July parade. The parades often included floats and marching bands. Note the sign for the Kneeskern store, located across the street from the D.H. Brown store. (Courtesy of Barbara Block.)

For many years, the Bridgeport Opera House, later called the Bridgeport Playhouse, was the center of summer entertainment in the area. Both local and traveling companies performed productions on the stage. This 1800s structure was the original home of the Baptist church. It was located next to a building first used as classrooms for kindergarten through second grade, which later became a hardware store with several owners over the years. (Courtesy of Dawn Pindle Falge.)

This is the cover of the program for a show called *The Late Christopher Bean*. The program tells about the play and is full of advertisements for local businesses. This play was performed at 8:45 p.m. November 26–28, 1948. (Courtesy of Rose [Myers] Fischer.)

Many summer productions at the Bridgeport Playhouse were performed by traveling companies of actors and actresses. These three women were in one of the productions. The visitors usually boarded in houses along Route 31. (Courtesy of Dawn Pindle Falge.)

This is the program for what was billed as the *Gay Nineties Revue*. It was held at the Bridgeport Playhouse in 1948. The Bridgeport Mother's Club tried to include many people from the community in these productions, usually as a way to raise funds to help the schools. (Courtesy of the Bridgeport Mother's Club.)

Gay Nineties Revue

Presented By

The Mother's Club

of

BRIDGEPORT, N. Y.

BRIDGEPORT PLAYHOUSE

NOVEMBER 26, 1948
+ 28

The cast of the *Gay Nineties Revue* is seen below. Very young children, older men and women, and a couple of seniors participated. June Marte was the coordinator and teacher for the dance numbers. It must have taken a lot of rehearsing and cooperation to put this show on successfully. (Courtesy of the Bridgeport Mother's Club.)

The *Gay Nineties Revue* included a chorus line of members of the Bridgeport Mother's Club. Coordinating the dance steps and moving the umbrellas could not have been easy. The Mother's Club began in 1947, and its activities were eventually turned over to the Bridgeport Parent-Teacher Association. (Courtesy of the Bridgeport Mother's Club.)

In 1954, the Bridgeport Mother's Club put an *Old Time Show*. Irene Snyder (left) and Shirley Pooley are seen here warming up backstage to do their act. Wearing that much makeup is a way to do funny things without revealing one's identity. (Courtesy of the Bridgeport Mother's Club.)

Lu Stewart, a famous local actress of this era, is seen here on stage before a show. She is likely preparing for a song, a dance, or perhaps even joke telling. She was a well-loved show participant. The show was performed on the stage of the new Bridgeport School. (Courtesy of the Bridgeport Mother's Club.)

Children are dressed for Halloween trick-or-treating in this Bridgeport photograph. The hotel on the corner of Route 31 and Bridgeport Kirkville Road still has double porches at this time, and the children certainly have on fancy costumes. (Courtesy of Patricia Hogan.)

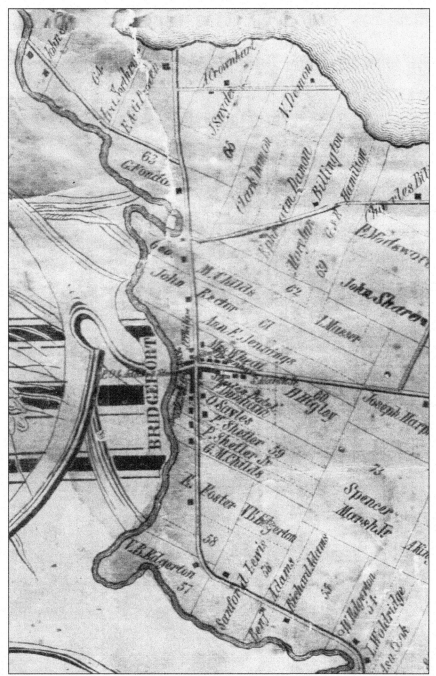

This map is a copy of the Gordon Evans map of 1853. It comes from the *Atlas of Madison County, New York*, published by Pomeroy, Whitman & Co. of Philadelphia in 1875. The Jennings and Rector family names on the map are cited in other histories as names of very early settlers. The names Damon and Billington seen here were well known among early residents. A few of the homes from these two families still exist. The lines on the left side of the creek are design lines by the mapmaker and do not indicate property or road names that would have been in Onandaga County at this time. (Courtesy of Sandra Bushnell Wilsey.)

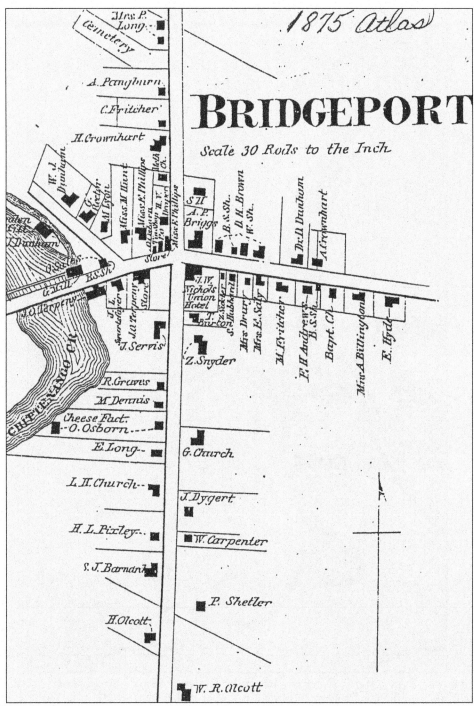

This map also comes from *Atlas of Madison County*. The names of some of the property owners on the map have changed, so the date has to have been later than 1853. The names Briggs and Brown were those of early business owners. The J.W. Nichols Union Hotel building is still a bar and restaurant, now called the Union, with the date 1856 on its sign. With a bridge across it, the creek is clearly close to some of the buildings. (Courtesy of Sandra Bushnell Wilsey.)

It is unknown when this drawing was created, and it is also difficult to read the artist's name. For many years, locals recall that a copy of it hung on the wall at Bottings Hotel and Grill. People also remember Ted Botting handing out copies to his bar and dining room customers. Whoever drew it certainly knew a lot about old-time Bridgeport. Even the sketches of the residents from way back then look very much like the actual people. (Courtesy of Ted Botting.)

Visit us at
arcadiapublishing.com

CPSIA information can be obtained
at www.ICGtesting.com
Printed in the USA
BVOW03*0330010617
485754BV00010B/38/P

9 781531 672713